I Am

Walt Disney

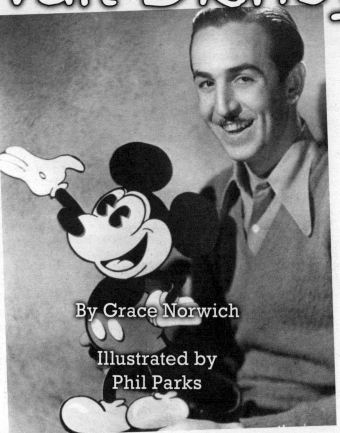

By Grace Norwich

Illustrated by
Phil Parks

SCHOLASTIC INC.

PHOTO CREDITS

Photographs © 2014: Dreamstime: 36 (Moritorus), 120; Everett Collection: 65; Getty Images: 14, 18, 81 (Apic), 77 (Earl Theisen), 84 (Fritz Goro/Time & Life Pictures), 86 (Galerie Bilderwelt), 40 (Gamma-Rapho), 97 (Gene Lester/Archive Photos), 12, 62 (Hulton Archive), 4 (J.R. Eyerman/Time Life Pictures), 46 (William Vanderson/Fox Photos); iStockphoto: 99 (Ina Peters), 110 (JodiJacobson), 88 (Joesboy), 113 (Razvan), 122 (Tom Young); Library of Congress: 21, 26, 33, 72, 79, 82, 85, 92, 102; Photofest: 53, 66, 70, 75 (Walt Disney Pictures), 1, 43, 58; Shutterstock, Inc.: 91 (James Steidl), 90 (Jonathan Tichon), film strips throughout (Kjpargeter), 17 (M.M.), film border throughout (Petrov Stanislav), 57 (Vacclav), 89 (Vuk Vukmirovic); The Granger Collection: 50 (Ewing Galloway/Published by 'Koralle' 1932/ Vintage property of ullstein bild), 69; Thinkstock: 35, 45 (iStockphoto), 54 (PhotoObjects.net), 106 (Top Photo Group); VectorStock/Sky_Max: photo border throughout; Wikipedia/Macfadden Publications: 101.

ISBN 978-0-545-62918-8

10 9 8 7   16 17 18 19/0

Printed in the U.S.A.   40
First printing, January 2014

Cover illustration by Mark Fredrickson
Interior illustrations by Phil Parks

CONTENTS

INTRODUCTION

Without me, Walt Disney, there would be no Mickey Mouse. There would be no Donald Duck, Goofy, or Pluto, either. I was a pioneer in the world of **animation**. Animation is a running series of pictures that creates the **illusion** of movement—like a flip-book. I was one of the first people to pair animation with sound to make what we recognize today as cartoons. I expanded my cartoons to create the first full-length animated movie in America, *Snow White and the Seven Dwarfs*. I went on to make many more beloved movies such as *Fantasia*, *Bambi*, *Cinderella*, and *Peter Pan*. To top it all off, I created Disneyland—one of the largest and most incredible amusement parks in the world. There had been amusement parks before I built Disneyland, but nothing else could compare. When it opened, Disneyland covered 160 sprawling acres in Anaheim, California. I set out to design something "like nothing else in the world" and Disneyland delivered. So did the other Disney parks that came later, like Walt Disney World in Orlando, Florida, where its Magic Kingdom has an amazing replica of Cinderella's castle from the 1950 movie. Walt Disney World also has Epcot, which boasts an eighteen-story structure shaped like a sphere. Inside is an attraction known as Spaceship Earth, which takes visitors on a tour through

achievements in human communication such as the alphabet and the printing press—from prehistoric man to the digital age.

My legacy as one of the world's greatest entertainers lives on today. The Walt Disney Company continues to make blockbuster movies like *The Little Mermaid* and *The Lion King*. And there are now eleven theme parks worldwide that bear my name!

I believed in the power of imagination and I worked hard to bring my ideas to life. I gave Mickey Mouse his trademark laugh and I made Tinker Bell light up the screen. I am Walt Disney.

PEOPLE YOU WILL MEET

WALT DISNEY

One of the most influential entertainers of the twentieth century. The man behind Mickey Mouse, Donald Duck, and scores of other timeless characters, as well as groundbreaking movies like *Snow White and the Seven Dwarfs.*

Elias Disney: Walt's father, who demanded much of his children even as he struggled throughout his life to hold down a job.

Flora Disney: Walt's mother, who was encouraging and more even-tempered than Elias.

Roy Disney: Walt had three older brothers—Herbert, Ray, and Roy. Roy protected Walt and remained devoted to him throughout his life. Walt and Roy founded the Disney Brothers Cartoon Studio together.

 **Walt Pfeiffer:** One of Walt Disney's best friends from childhood. Walt D. and Walt P. developed a comedy act they named "The Two Walts."

 **Ub Iwerks:** A fellow artist who served as Walt's first business partner and was the first cartoonist to draw Mickey Mouse.

 **Margaret Winkler:** A leading distributor of cartoons in the 1920s who gave Walt his first break by offering to buy his Alice in Wonderland animated shorts.

 **Lillian Bounds:** An artist hired by Walt who became his wife in 1925.

 **Diane and Sharon Disney:** Walt and Lillian's two daughters, who enjoyed life with a doting dad who built a miniature railroad in their backyard!

TIME LINE

- **August 1834** – Walt Disney's great-grandfather emigrates to the United States from Ireland.

- **December 5, 1901** – Walt Disney is born.

- **1906** – The Disneys move to Marceline, Missouri.

- **1911** – The Disneys move to Kansas City, Missouri.

- **1922** – Disney starts Laugh-O-gram Films, Inc.

- **1923** – Disney moves to Hollywood, California.

- **1925** – Walt and Lillian Bounds get married.

- **1927** – Walt and Ub Iwerks come up with Oswald the Lucky Rabbit.

- **1928** – Walt loses the rights to Oswald to a rival, who takes Walt's animators as well.

- **1928** – Walt creates Mickey Mouse.

- **November 18, 1928** – *Steamboat Willie* is shown for the first time in New York City.

- **1933** – *The Three Little Pigs* premieres; Walt and Lillian have a daughter, Diane.

- **1936** – Walt and Lillian adopt a baby girl named Sharon.

- **January 13, 1938** – *Snow White and the Seven Dwarfs* opens at Radio City Music Hall in New York City.

- **1940–1953** – Walt leads production on *Pinocchio, Fantasia, Dumbo, Bambi, Cinderella, Treasure Island, Alice in Wonderland,* and *Peter Pan* as well as many other movies.

- **1954** – Walt creates the *Disneyland* TV show on ABC and appears as its host.

- **July 17, 1955** – Walt opens Disneyland in Anaheim, California.

- **1965** – Walt buys nearly 30,000 acres of land in Florida for Walt Disney World and Epcot.

- **December 15, 1966** – Walt dies from lung cancer.

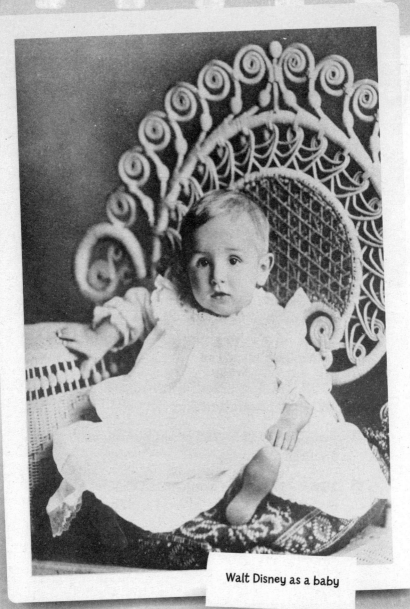

Walt Disney as a baby

CHAPTER ONE

NOT EXACTLY A STORYBOOK CHILDHOOD

For all the joy that Walt Disney spread around the world, you might assume he had a happy, carefree childhood. In fact, Walt's early years were often a struggle.

He was born Walter Elias Disney on December 5, 1901, in Chicago, Illinois. His parents, Elias and Flora, were hard workers and active churchgoers. They ran a strict household where a strong work ethic was more important than having fun.

Elias worked as a builder at the time, which

Disney's parents, Flora and Elias

was a tough way to make a living. The family often had trouble making ends meet. Flora was forced to do construction work with her husband because they needed money so badly.

By the time Walt, a blond, delicate-featured child, was born, the Disneys already had three other mouths to feed: Herbert, Raymond, and Roy. Two years after Walt was born, a baby girl named Ruth came along. In a search for better jobs, the Disney family moved every few years when Walt was a kid. Elias took them from the city to the country, and then to a different city years later.

Walt's stern father, Elias, didn't display a lot of emotion except for anger. He had a bad temper, and lots of things set him off. He didn't approve of drinking, dancing, or silliness. Elias cared for his family, but it wasn't easy being his son.

Life on the Farm

In 1906 the Disney clan moved to Marceline, a town in the middle of rural Missouri. The children were all excited to live on a farm. The Disneys lived in a one-story wooden farmhouse surrounded by forty-five acres of farmland and orchards boasting "every kind of apple you ever heard of," as Walt described. The area was filled with small animals and birds. The natural surroundings were a great escape for the Disney children from their difficult home life. In summer, they fished for catfish and went swimming in the local creek with the other children in the neighborhood. In winter, they would sled down to the creek and skate on its frozen surface.

Even five-year-old Walt had responsibilities on the farm. His job was to watch out for the pigs and make sure they didn't get into trouble. One of the pigs seemed to take a shine to Walt.

Disney grew up in a farmhouse surrounded by an orchard, similar to the one in this photograph.

Walt and his sister, Ruth

Her name was Skinny, and she would wander over to the house looking for him. Walt loved all the animals on the farm and made sure to say hello to each one every morning as he went out to the barn to start his chores. These early experiences inspired his later work.

Walt didn't go to school until he was seven. The other siblings and his parents were too busy to take him, so they just kept him at home until his little sister was old enough to go to school, too. The late start didn't bother Walt much. He didn't care much for studies, although he liked the opportunities to make his classmates laugh.

Walt was not a very good student in school. Instead of studying, he passed the time drawing flip-books in the corners of his notebooks. Flip-books are a series of pictures that change slightly from one to the next so that when you flip the pages, it looks like animation.

Marceline Magic

Walt's lifelong love of trains began with Marceline. The Missouri town existed because of the railroad boom. To connect Chicago to the West, the railroad company had to create small towns every hundred miles along the route so that workers would have places to live, and trains would be able to get serviced if they broke down. Marceline, where Walt first watched the play *Peter Pan*, helped inspire Disneyland's idealized Main Street, U.S.A.

Walt loved trains just like this one from around 1900.

A Young Artist

Walt's uncle Robert was much more successful than his older brother Elias. Whenever Robert visited, he acted like he owned the farm. He managed to annoy everyone and he treated Elias with very little respect. But Walt was always happy to see him—particularly because Uncle Robert's wife, Aunt Margaret, brought him drawing paper and pencils as a gift. Walt wanted to draw ever since he was old enough to hold a pencil, but Aunt Margaret was the first one to encourage him.

An older neighbor, Doc Sherwood, also gave Walt a lot of praise for his art. It was an important relationship, since Walt didn't really fit in at home. He was a rowdy, charming little boy who loved having fun. His behavior did not always go over so well with his strict father.

Doc Sherwood was well respected in town.

He let Walt ride in his buggy with him as he ran errands or visited sick people. He told the little boy never to be afraid to admit he didn't know something. Walt asked Doc Sherwood all kinds of questions. Doc answered with patience, which was so different from Walt's easily irritated dad. Doc also did something that would stay with Walt for the rest of his life. One day he asked Walt to draw him a picture of his stallion, Rupert. The horse wouldn't stay still, so Walt had to keep moving around to keep the animal's head in profile. The result was awful, but he treasured the memory of being asked to draw something.

Walt's artistic efforts, however, were not always appreciated. After he found a barrel of soft black tar on the farm, he decided to use it as paint and draw on the side of the family house. But the tar never came off! Walt's parents were not pleased.

Doc Sherwood asked Walt to
draw his stallion, Rupert.

Good-bye to Farm Life

The Disney family was forced to move again in 1911 because Elias was not able to make a profit on the farm. He stubbornly refused to use fertilizer until it became clear that his crops really needed it. He also didn't know how to take care of his animals properly. Things got so bad that the family couldn't heat their home. Flora had to send the boys to bed with heated bricks to put in the blankets so they wouldn't freeze! Still, Walt was sad to leave Marceline and life on the farm.

Amusement park roller
coaster from around 1900

CHAPTER TWO

NEXT STOP KANSAS CITY

After failing in Marceline, Elias set his sights on the larger Midwest metropolis of Kansas City, Missouri. The Disneys moved into a house so small that Walt and his brother Roy had to sleep in a shed in the backyard when guests stayed the night. Not only was the house small, it lacked indoor plumbing! But there was one upside. It was right near an amusement park. Walt and Ruth were forbidden from going, but that didn't keep them from standing outside the gates to look.

Walt worked as a paperboy delivering the *Kansas City Star*.

A Hardworking Paperboy

Elias bought a paper route for one of the biggest newspapers in Kansas City, the *Kansas City Star.* He hired a team of boys to deliver the papers, including Roy and Walt. But while all the other boys got paid three dollars a week, Walt didn't make a penny. At just nine years old, Walt had a full share of responsibility in the business. He delivered papers in the morning before six a.m., came home for a nap, and then got up and went to school. He left school half an hour early every day so that he could be on time to pick up the evening papers and start deliveries. He had another job delivering medicine for a local pharmacy to earn pocket money. He also managed to

Elias Disney

convince Elias to let him have more papers to sell on the trolley! Life was busy for young Walt.

Delivering papers wasn't any easier than farming. In the winter, Walt slipped and fell on icy steps while trudging through snow up to his knees. He was so tired in the early mornings that he sometimes fell asleep inside apartment house lobbies or curled up inside the newspaper sack. Those naps meant he had to run the rest of the way to complete his route.

In the winter of 1916, Walt kicked a piece of ice and accidentally impaled his foot with a nail that was frozen inside the ice. It took twenty minutes of screaming for help before a deliveryman found and took him to a doctor, who pulled out the nail with a pair of pliers and gave him a shot. Even though he told people later that he thought the paper route gave him a very strong work ethic, he had nightmares about it for the rest of his life.

As an adult, Walt had nightmares about his tough job as a paperboy.

The Two Bad Walters

Home life had never been good for the Disneys. But it went from bad to worse in Kansas City. Elias's temper was often directed at Walt, who resented the control his father had over his life. Tensions between Elias and Walt continued to grow until they got into a physical fight. Walt, who was fourteen years old, grabbed his father's hands to keep Elias from hitting him with a hammer. When Walt finally stood up to his father, Elias broke down and began to cry.

Walt Pfeiffer

Fortunately, Walt had a full life outside of his home, including lots of friends. One of his best buddies was another Walt, Walt Pfeiffer. When Walt P. had the mumps, Walt Disney told Mrs. Pfeiffer not to worry. Walt D. had been sick with the mumps before, too. He kept Pfeiffer company while he was sick and taught him how to draw.

The Pfeiffers lived down the street, and Walt D. would go up to bed at night and then climb out his window so that he could go to their house. Obsessed with Charlie Chaplin, the boys started performing comedy routines at school

English comedy actor Charlie Chaplin started his career as a child performer. He became one of the biggest stars of the silent-film era with his iconic bowler hat, mustache, and cane.

and in talent shows. They named their act the "The Two Walts."

From Comedy to Cartoons

Despite dabbling in theater, Walt never lost his passion for drawing. In school, he propped his books up on his desk so that he could draw behind them. This wasn't exactly model pupil behavior, but instead of punishing him, his teacher Daisy Beck asked him to draw posters for events at school. Walt's talent attracted attention and soon he was earning money for his work. He drew advertisements for a local theater. Walt was also paid in haircuts by the owner of a barbershop near his house for his cartoons. The owner hung Walt's drawings in the shop window, rotating them out once a week or so. People started going to the barbershop specifically to see Walt's artwork each week!

Art supplies—just like ones Walt would have used at the Chicago Institute of Art

Walt drew all kinds of things. He figured out how to **mimic** the style of the political cartoons in his father's newspapers. He practiced until he had the style down perfectly. To further his talents, he started taking art classes at the

Kansas City Art Institute when he was fourteen. Elias let him go, even though he didn't know anything about art and didn't understand Walt's talent at all.

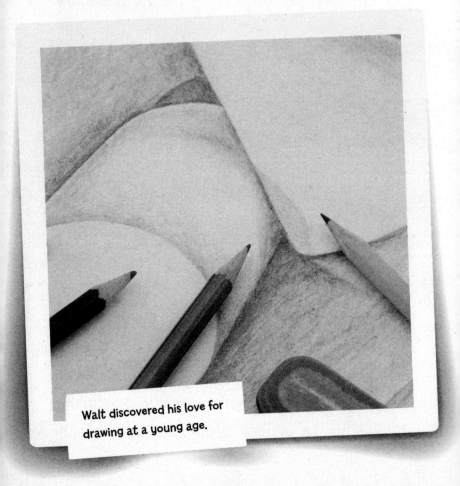

Walt discovered his love for drawing at a young age.

When the Disneys moved to Chicago in 1917, Walt took art classes at the Chicago Institute of Art three evenings a week. He persuaded Elias to give him the money for art classes by saying it was an educational experience. He was fascinated by working with live models, but his favorite course at the academy was taught by a cartoonist at the *Chicago Herald*. Walt's talents were so obvious that after only a month at McKinley High School he became the school magazine's cartoonist.

Walt to War

In the summer of 1918, Walt and a friend tried to join the navy to fight in World War I, but as seventeen-year-olds they were too young. After the Canadian military rejected them as well, they became ambulance drivers since the age requirement was seventeen. At first Elias and Flora refused to let him go, but Walt finally got his mother to sign papers certifying his age.

The war itself was over by the time Walt got to France. Still, he was put to work driving supplies, soldiers, and officials in its aftermath. Walt became a very good tour guide and was in demand by the time he left the country. He kept up his drawing—and his bank account—by charging soldiers a fee to draw caricatures for them to send back home to their families and girlfriends.

By the time Walt got home in October 1919, he was convinced he wanted to become an artist no matter how much the idea horrified his father.

Walt drove an ambulance
in France after World War I.

Walt and his
brother Roy

CHAPTER THREE

WALT'S FIRST JOB IN FILM

Walt knew that his father would never truly support his desire to be an artist, so he moved from Chicago back to Kansas City where his brother Roy was living. Walt got a job through one of Roy's friends, working as an assistant for two commercial artists named Louis Pesmen and Bill Rubin. At that job, he met a man with a nice face and a very strange name—Ub Iwerks—and the two became friends. The work wasn't that creative, but Walt was happy to be getting paid to draw. Unfortunately, Lou and Bill had to fire both men after the advertising rush at Christmas ended, and Walt was forced to get a job delivering mail in order to earn money.

Walt and Ub: Business Partners

Ub Iwerks was panicked about how he was going to support himself and his mother after being laid off. He paid Walt a visit a few weeks after their dismissal. Although Walt's father had failed at so many businesses in his life, perhaps his willingness to try different jobs sparked Walt's **entrepreneurial** spirit. Walt decided that he and Ub should go into business together. Iwerks was shocked, but Walt was off and running! Iwerks gave Walt some sample artwork and Walt began looking for clients. Walt also wrote his parents, asking them to send him the money he'd saved up over the years. Flora only sent him half his savings, but that was enough

Ub Iwerks was Walt's
trusted business partner.

to get the firm of Iwerks-Disney off the ground.
(Iwerks got his name first in the title because the
other way around sounded like they performed
eye exams!) Walt and Ub created illustrations
for the newspaper *Restaurant News* in exchange
for office space for their new company.

Walt worked as an artist for the Kansas City Slide Company.

Although business was good from the start, Iwerks encouraged Walt to apply for an opening as an artist at the Kansas City Slide Company, which created the slides that were shown in movie theaters before the main show. Walt not only applied but landed the job at the largest mail-order slide firm in the country!

Walt was put to work creating animated picture advertisements, mainly using stop-motion animation. Following this technique, he

Walt didn't forget about his good pal Iwerks! Walt got Ub a job as an artist at the slide company, and they closed down Iwerks-Disney for good.

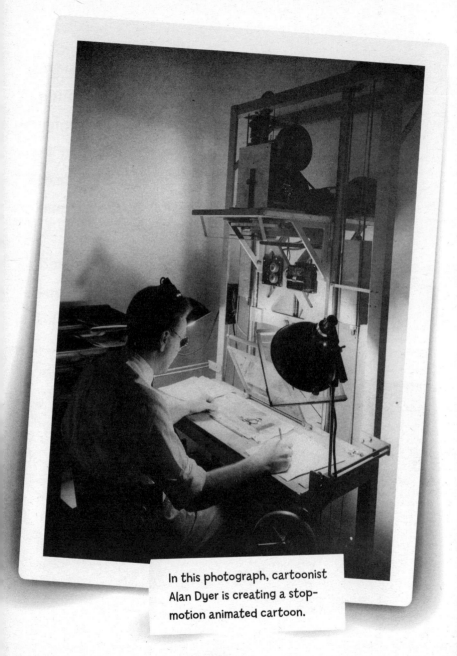

In this photograph, cartoonist Alan Dyer is creating a stop-motion animated cartoon.

and his colleagues would draw pictures and cut out any elements that were supposed to move. They would then pin the cutouts to a board, take a picture, move them a little, take a picture, and repeat the process until the entire ad was contained in the still frames. The individual pictures were used to create a film strip. As a film strip, all the pictures would flow together and create the impression of motion. Although the process was clunky, Walt turned down another job offer as a cartoonist at one of the big city papers to stay at the Kansas City Slide Company. Walt had fallen in love with animation.

CHAPTER FOUR

WALT FINDS HIS TRUE CALLING

Stop-motion had introduced Walt to the magic of animation, but he knew there were greater possibilities beyond the rough, sometimes clumsy pictures he was creating at the slide company.

One of these possibilities was a new **innovation** called cel animation, which had been developed by a film director named Earl Hurd in 1913. Cel animation is named after the sheets of **celluloid** on which Hurd drew images.

An artist is working on a cartoon of Mickey Mouse using cel animation.

He'd paint the background on one sheet of **transparent** celluloid, then draw the characters that moved on a second transparent sheet laid on top. This process eliminated the need to redraw the background of each scene. Only the moving parts had to be redrawn for each frame.

Laugh-O-grams

Walt was eager to learn the new technology, mostly being used in New York City, even if he had to do so on his own. So that's just what he did, with help from a book by Carl Lutz called *Animated Cartoons: How They Are Made, Their Origin and Development*. His first studio was in his parents' small garage.

Using a camera he convinced his boss at the slide company to lend him, Walt spent all his free time in the garage, practicing this new art long after everyone else had gone to sleep. He managed to create some pretty funny animated

How Cartoons Are Made

It takes 14,000 drawings to make a traditional animated film that lasted just ten minutes. When computer-generated imagery, or CGI, was created, the animation process changed dramatically. Disney's *Toy Story*, the first fully computer-generated animated film, was created in 1995. The current Disney animation companies no longer do very many hand-drawn films.

Toy Story was the first movie to be animated entirely using CGI.

short films, called shorts, and took them to a man named Frank Newman, who owned several movie theaters. Walt called his shorts Newman's Laugh-O-grams, and Newman loved them.

Walt's Laugh-O-grams were so good that in the spring of 1922, he started his own company, Laugh-O-gram Films, Inc., and persuaded Iwerks to join him. He also hired a high-school

Laugh-O-grams were only about a minute or two long. Some gave instructions about how to act properly in a movie theatre—just like some of the short movies that we see today before feature films. But the advice to viewers has changed! In one Laugh-O-gram, a cartoon professor warns moviegoers not to read the titles of silent films out loud or else he will hit them over the head with a large mallet.

student and a couple of other young men, but told them up front that he couldn't pay them. Employees would only earn money if their cartoons did. The office environment at Laugh-O-gram Films was fun and creative. The workers made up jokes for the shorts, drew characters, and used a movie camera to bring their ideas to life.

A Good, Hard Failure

Unfortunately, it seemed Walt had inherited some of his father's bad business sense. Although he had trouble finding buyers for his cartoons, that didn't stop him from hiring more people and acting on new ideas. His finances were so bad at times that Walt and his fellow animators went without food, and a few times Walt had to move in with Iwerks. They had to sneak their equipment out of the office more than once when they couldn't afford to pay rent.

Eventually, Walt had to face reality and let all his employees go.

In debt and miserable, Walt caught a break when a dentist hired him to draw a cartoon that taught children how to take care of their teeth. Still, the paycheck wasn't enough to save his business. With nothing keeping him in Kansas City, Walt sold his camera, put a single change of clothes in a suitcase, and headed for a place where he knew there was a much better chance of success—Hollywood.

"I'd failed," Walt said later. "I think it's important to have a good, hard failure when you're young. I learned a lot out of that." True to his words, his hard failure would lead to wild success, but not before he overcame his fair share of **adversity**.

Walt moves to Hollywood—
seen here is the classic movie
town sign.

Walt Disney poses with
Mickey Mouse in this
photo from around 1930.

CHAPTER FIVE

MOVIES, MARRIAGE, AND A MOUSE NAMED MICKEY

Walt might not have been the best businessman during the early days of his career, but he always had plenty of charisma. So when he finally reached Hollywood in August of 1923, one of the first things he did was talk his way into the major movie studios. Universal Pictures, Warner Bros., and Paramount operated within their own lots—a group of buildings that house movie sets. Multiple films were all shot at the same time in different locations around the studio lots. Walt walked through the lots and watched the movies being filmed. He was so curious he often stayed until late at night.

Walt's Big Break

Next he had to talk his way into an actual job at a studio. To show people what he could do, he used a short film he'd made at Laugh-O-gram based on *Alice's Adventures in Wonderland*, about a real little girl who went into another world where she could play with cartoon animals. He sent it to a woman named Margaret Winkler. Only twenty-eight at the time, Winkler was already one of the leading cartoon distributors in the country—and the

Margaret Winkler

only woman. She liked the short and wrote Walt to say she was interested in buying a series of shorts.

Here was the big break Walt had been waiting for! He couldn't blow it. As he did

Roy Disney

throughout his life, he turned to his big brother Roy for support. Walt convinced Roy to go into business with him. Roy agreed and Disney Brothers Studio was born, altering the course of history forever.

Roy handled the business side of things, which allowed Walt the freedom to work on the animations. The company, renamed The Walt Disney Studios, had twelve employees including Ub Iwerks, who had followed Walt to yet another job. Also at the studio was a young woman named Lillian Bounds, who did "ink and

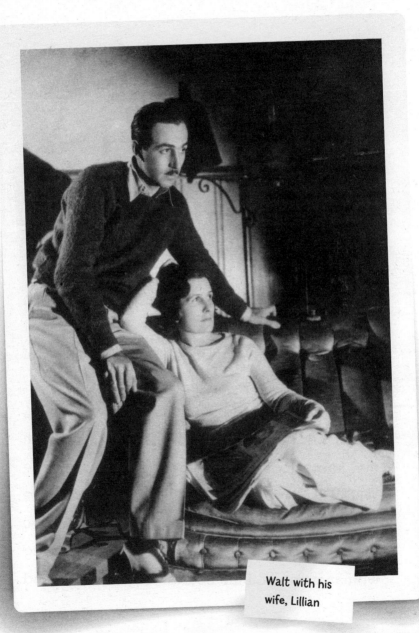

Walt with his
wife, Lillian

paint," a common job for women in animation at the time. For fifteen dollars per week, she took the animators' drawings and painted them onto the transparent cels that would be used to create the animation.

Lillian Bounds

Small and dark-haired, Lillian was a lot of fun to be around. Walt drove her and another woman home from work every night instead of letting them walk or wait for a bus. After a while, Lillian noticed he always dropped the other girl off first. He wouldn't come in and meet her family, though, because he didn't own a suit. He did get one a little while later, and a few months after that, he proposed to Lillian by asking if she thought he should buy himself a new car or her an engagement ring. What a gentleman!

Double-Crossed!

The animation team at The Walt Disney Studios had nearly fifty Alice movies (each about seven minutes long) when Margaret Winkler and Charles Mintz, her partner and new husband, told them that they wanted an all-cartoon series—as opposed to the Alice series, which was a combination of **live action** and animation. Walt and Ub worked hard and came up with Oswald the Lucky Rabbit. Oswald was an instant hit because of its superior animation and the humor of the mischievous rabbit. Oswald's adventures were chronicled in twenty-six shorts. Everything was going well until Walt took a trip to New York to ask Mintz for a raise. While he was there, he learned that Mintz had sold the rights for Oswald to Universal Pictures. Universal now controlled all the profits from the character that Walt thought he owned. Mintz had also signed separate contracts with most

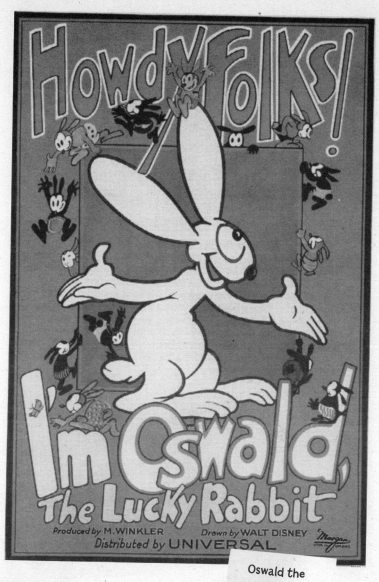

Oswald the
Lucky Rabbit

of Walt's staff—he wanted them to work for him directly instead of Walt. "Take the staff!" he shouted at Mintz in anger.

To save his studio, which was basically only Iwerks after Mintz lured the rest of the staff away, Walt needed a new character. On the train ride back from New York, depressed and angry,

Mickey Mouse was the star of Walt's first cartoon with sound.

he thought up a character, a mouse named Mortimer. "By the time the train had reached the Middle West, I had dressed my dream mouse in a pair of velvet pants and two huge pearl buttons," Walt said. He told Lillian about Mortimer. She loved the idea but not the name. Eventually, they settled on the name Mickey.

Mickey Is Born!

When they got back to California, Walt, Iwerks, Roy, and Lillian started work on the new character. Walt wrote the script, Iwerks drew like crazy, and Lillian inked the drawings. Walt had a hard time selling the first Mickey cartoons. He needed a new angle, but what?

In 1927, the first live-action movie to have its own sound (instead of just a musical **accompaniment**) came out. *The Jazz Singer*, starring Al Jolson, was a **revelation** to Walt, who decided he wanted to add sound to his Mickey

The Mickey Mouse Club's Beginnings

To get more kids to come to his Ocean Park, California, movie theater, the manager came up with the idea for a "Mickey Mouse Club." He invited young people to special showings of Mickey Mouse cartoons and other events like pie-eating contests. When Walt saw how excited so many children were over Mickey Mouse, he thought it would be a good idea to start other chapters of the Mickey Mouse Club in cities all over the country. At the height of its popularity, there were more than a million members nationwide!

Mickey Mouse cartoon poster from 1929

Audiences loved Mickey
Mouse in the cartoon
Steamboat Willie.

Mouse cartoons. He envisioned the sound happening **in sync** with the action on the screen. He and his small team created *Steamboat Willie*, sold it, and in November 1928, it was shown in New York for the first time at the Colony Theater to immediate **acclaim**. Soon, in addition to a Mickey Mouse comic strip, there were all kinds of Mickey merchandise. Producers from many different studios wanted Walt to make Mickey Mouse cartoons for them, but Walt refused every offer. After the episode with Mintz, Walt vowed never to lose control of one of his characters again.

During the Great Depression many families, like this one, struggled in poverty.

CHAPTER SIX

MASTER OF INNOVATION

In 1929, the United States economy declined and a terrible period called the Great Depression began. Many people lost their jobs, and many families struggled in poverty. But movies were one of the few forms of escape from the hardship and misery of the bad economic situation. The timing was perfect for Mickey Mouse, and Walt's earnings offered him a taste of true financial freedom.

He could have kicked back and relaxed.

Instead, Walt looked for ways for his studio to get bigger and better. He focused on helping his art staff improve their skills, and even hired art teachers to give classes after work. He paid for his artists to have dinner before attending evening art class.

Walt's Next Big Experiment

As his staff became more skilled, Walt started working on Silly Symphonies, a series of cartoons that let them play around with different ways of telling stories and animating them. Walt always wanted to be innovating. He was excited by Technicolor, which allowed movies and cartoons to be shown in color instead of black-and-white. In 1932, Walt used the technology for a cartoon called *Flowers and Trees,* which was about trees falling in love. It got so much praise that it went on to become the first cartoon to win an Academy Award.

Walt's cartoon *Three Little Pigs* won an Academy Award.

For Walt's next big experiment, he wanted to create a longer cartoon with a more complex plot and more recognizable characters. He decided on *Three Little Pigs*, which would win another Academy Award. The film's song "Who's Afraid of the Big Bag Wolf?" became the biggest hit in the country.

Diane and Sharon

Even as Walt was busy creating award-winning masterpieces, he and Lillian found time to start a family. Lillian gave birth to a daughter, Diane Marie, in December 1933. Three years later, in 1936, Walt and Lillian adopted a baby girl they named Sharon.

It was an incredibly busy time for Walt, who by all accounts was a huge success. And yet, he still wasn't making as much money as he needed to in order to keep the studio going. It had grown considerably since he started out, and by this time he employed 750 people. However, the cartoons kept getting more expensive to produce as the technology got more sophisticated. Movie theater owners had started running double features—two movies

Walt with his daughters,
Diane and Sharon

for the price of one—and while that kept their theaters full, it meant that they didn't have enough money to rent short cartoons.

Snow White Becomes a Movie Star

Walt decided this was the time to make yet another innovation he'd been thinking about for a while: a full-length animated movie. He picked the story of Snow White, based on the fairy tale by the Brothers Grimm. He grabbed his key artists and sat them down after work one night to act out *his* version of Snow White. Walt made a practice of acting out his ideas as he explained them.

Walt innovated using sound when he made *Steamboat Willie* and full Technicolor when he created *Three Little Pigs* and *Flowers and Trees*. He continued experimenting and innovating to bring *Snow White* to life.

Snow White was very expensive to make. Walt thought he'd need half a million dollars,

Radio City
Music Hall

but the studio ended up borrowing over $1.5 million by the time they were done. Although Walt went way over budget, he got a fairy-tale ending. After its opening at Radio City Music Hall in New York City on January 13, 1938, *Snow White and the Seven Dwarfs* made $8.5 million—a huge amount of money when you consider that adult movie tickets were twenty-five cents and children's tickets were a dime!

The Multiplane Camera

Walt wanted *Snow White* to be realistic enough to hold viewers' attention for the length of a full feature film. That meant he had to figure out a way to overcome the lack of depth in traditional animation. Enter another Disney creation: the multiplane camera. Walt's innovation used techniques from live theater where scenery—flat cutouts of anything from trees to buildings—is placed in varying layers in front of a backdrop so that when actors move through the set pieces they look to the audience like they are moving through forests, into villages, or any other kind of space. Based on the same idea, the multiplane camera shot through up to five different planes. The first two planes were for the moving characters, the next two for the backgrounds, and the fifth plane was for sky. The whole thing was very costly and difficult, but the end result was an animated film more lifelike than anyone had ever seen before.

Snow White and the
Seven Dwarfs

Main gate of The Walt
Disney Studios, casting
building, Burbank, L.A.

CHAPTER SEVEN

GROWING PAINS FOR THE DISNEY EMPIRE

By 1940, Disney had more than a thousand employees in a new fifty-one-acre studio complex in Burbank, California. Each department, from accounting to animation, had its own building.

After *Snow White*, the Disney team created a slew of full-length animated movies—*Pinocchio*, *Fantasia*, *Dumbo,* and *Bambi*—as well as some of the most recognizable cartoon characters such as Donald Duck, Pluto, and Goofy. Walt's studio had turned into an American institution.

Pinocchio was not an instant success. It cost over $2 million to make and it took many years to earn that money back. *Pinocchio* was released during the Second World War and was translated into fewer languages than *Snow White*. Both factors likely hurt the movie's earnings.

Walt Helps the War Effort

Despite The Walt Disney Company's many successes, it continued to struggle financially, especially after the start of World War II. Profits from Europe, which had always been a huge market for Disney, dried up as war raged across the continent. But Walt always took the studio's financial woes in stride. In fact, when Roy told him that they owed $4.5 million to the bank, his big brother was shocked when Walt responded

84

by laughing. "I was just thinking back when we couldn't borrow a thousand dollars."

On December 7, 1941, when Pearl Harbor was attacked by Japanese bombers, the war affected a lot more than Disney's bottom line. The Disney company partnered with the U.S. Army and

Japanese bomb
Pearl Harbor.

In this poster for Walt's cartoon to help the war effort, Donald Duck throws a tomato at Adolf Hitler.

allowed them to move an antiaircraft unit onto the Burbank studio grounds. Seven hundred soldiers, fourteen trucks, and lots of equipment moved into the studio complex. But that wasn't the last of Disney's involvement during WWII. Soon the studio began making training films for the armed forces. Walt even made cartoons to support the war effort, including several starring Donald Duck.

Animals as Actors

After the war ended, Walt turned his focus to another kind of danger threatening America: its vanishing nature. Worried that the country's wild lands were rapidly disappearing, he sent the husband-and-wife team of Alfred and Elma Milotte into Alaska to film anything and everything. Out of all the film they captured, from indigenous people to vast forests, Walt was captivated most by the seals on the Pribilof

Seals like this one from the Pribilof Island chain off of Alaska were the stars of *Seal Island*.

Islands off Alaska. The result was a **documentary** film called *Seal Island*, that broke the mold again because its main actors were animals! The company that distributed Disney's films didn't like the idea at all. They believed that audiences would be bored to tears by a movie about nature.

They couldn't have been more wrong. Not only did *Seal Island* win an Academy Award for Best Short Subject Film, but it launched the thirteen-film True-Life Adventures series. These movies were so powerful that when shown in public schools, they inspired students to go into the forestry service. *Seal Island* and the True-Life Adventures series paved the way for all the popular nature films we enjoy today.

The True-Life Adventure series helped make nature documentaries popular.

Censoring Nature

One of the True-Life Adventures movies, *Vanishing Prairie*, was banned in New York State when it came out in 1954 because it showed a buffalo giving birth. When Walt heard the news, he said, "It would be a shame if New York children had to believe the stork brings buffaloes, too."

The movie *Vanishing Prairie* showed a live buffalo birth.

Walt playfully poses with Mickey Mouse and a cat.

CHAPTER EIGHT

WALT LOOKS FOR OTHER FORMS OF AMUSEMENT

One of Walt's biggest sources of **inspiration** was his own children. Though he worked incredibly hard throughout his life, often putting in long hours at the office, he always remained a very devoted parent.

He often drove the girls each to their different schools every day before going to the studio. One time, he complained to his daughter's principal that the kids were assigned too much homework and didn't have enough time to be with their families.

Walt was disappointed
by the amusement
parks he saw.

Part of dad duty for Walt was taking his daughters, Diane and Sharon, to amusement parks where he walked around while the girls enjoyed the rides. While strolling, he took in the scenery and action, and what he saw wasn't pretty. The grounds were covered in litter and the kids seemed more bored than entertained. That got him thinking, and before long, he was busy cooking up an idea for an amusement park of his own. At first, he imagined putting it on the grounds of the Burbank studio. But as his ideas took shape, he realized that he would need much more space. Much, *much* more space!

Making the Perfect Park

Walt's ideal amusement park would never be finished. He wanted to build a park that could keep growing and developing. To get a project that grand in scope off the ground, he would need money.

Walt's Very Big Toy

Walt had always loved trains since his days in Marceline. When he, Lillian, and the girls were getting ready to move into a new, bigger house in the late 1940s, he wanted to buy a real (though scaled down) train for it. Lillian wasn't all that excited by the idea of a train running through her backyard, but that's exactly what she got. Walt named the engine the *Lilly Belle*, and even built some of the miniature railroad himself. When his daughters had friends over, he donned his engineer's cap, took them for a ride, and then made everyone huge banana split sundaes.

Walt driving friends in the
miniature train at his home

Even as Walt started planning the park in 1953, he had no idea how to raise the money he needed.

Walt's older brother Roy came up with a way to finance Walt's dream park. The answer, in a word: television. That might not seem like such a revolutionary idea today, but at the time, TV was still a relatively new medium. In fact, in 1953, only just over half of all homes in the United States owned a television.

Ever the **visionary**, Walt was convinced that there was going to be a lot of money in television. And of course, he was right. He made a deal with the American Broadcasting Company (ABC), one of the country's major television networks, to finance his park. In return, he would create television shows for ABC, including cartoons starring Mickey Mouse. The first program, *Disneyland*, hosted by Walt himself, was a runaway sensation. Next came the hit show

Even before TVs were popular, Roy Disney saw opportunity in TV programs.

Davy Crockett, a highly fictionalized miniseries about a real man who lived on the frontier in the 1800s. Another popular program was *The Mickey Mouse Club*, a variety show starring the Mouseketeers, a group of children who sang and danced on-screen.

The Mickey Mouse Club

The *Mickey Mouse Club* was a variety show for children that featured cartoons, music, dancing, comedy, and much more. The show aired on and off from 1955 to 1996. The show's performers were called Mouseketeers and many went on to become big stars, including Annette Funicello, Ryan Gosling, Justin Timberlake, Christina Aguilera, Britney Spears, and Keri Russell.

An early version of the Mouseketeers, featuring Annette Funicello, far left

The original entrance to Disneyland

Walt named the park he created Disneyland. It opened on July 17, 1955, just a few days before Walt and Lillian's thirtieth wedding anniversary. Walt loved designing the theme park and overseeing its construction. Diane remembered seeing her father literally move mountains at the under-construction theme park. He called the crews of people who designed and planned Disneyland his Imagineers.

Walt threw a huge party the night of July 13 with a guest list that ranged from his aunt Charlotte to Cary Grant, the famous movie star, and Louis Mayer, the former head of MGM Studios. The day before the park opened, Walt stayed up all night helping some of his employees create an exhibit to house the huge rubber squid from the film *20,000 Leagues Under the Sea.* Thirty thousand people came the first day. After the first three months, one million people had visited Walt's amazing theme park.

The public loved Disneyland. It was clean, it was safe, the rides were fun, and everything looked beautiful. Whether it was Adventureland, Fantasyland, Frontierland, or Tomorrowland, Walt had finally succeeded in turning the storybook childhood he never had into reality.

Walt's Disneyland

Walt liked to spend time in Disneyland, but he didn't want to attract attention. He would wear a big hat and sunglasses so he'd look like any other tourist. Once in a while a little kid would recognize him. When that happened, Walt just held a finger up to his lips and quietly gave the child an autograph. He spent a lot of time in Disneyland after the park was officially closed for the day, too. He even had a miniature fire engine that he drove through the streets, and a private apartment in the firehouse over Main Street.

Walt liked to visit Disneyland
without attracting attention.

Sleeping Beauty Castle
in Hong Kong Disneyland

CHAPTER NINE

UNFINISHED BUSINESS

The completion of Disneyland could have been a final highlight in Walt's already successful career. It certainly would have been a fitting cherry on top of a remarkable list of achievements that included more than eighty feature-length films and thirty-two Academy Awards. But Walt was far from finished. Even as he was wrapping up Disneyland, he played an integral role in the making of *Mary Poppins*. *Mary Poppins* was a movie that combined live-action and animation and starred Julie Andrews, an English stage actress with a beautiful singing voice. The movie received thirteen Academy Award nominations.

Walt Disney World

But the project that most excited Walt at this stage in his life was taking place across the country on thirty thousand acres of wilderness in Florida. This was where Walt had plans to build the biggest theme park the world had ever known: Walt Disney World.

The project became Walt's obsession. He didn't think of much else. Sure, he took days off here and there, including one in 1964 when President Lyndon Johnson awarded him the Presidential Medal of Freedom—the highest honor that can be given to a civilian by the US government. And of course Walt still made time for his family. He and Lillian often babysat for their grandchildren. He loved watching the kids build forts out of patio furniture in their backyard, and he also let them have sleepovers in Disneyland.

Otherwise, Walt was laser focused on Walt Disney World and especially the Experimental Prototype Community of Tomorrow (Epcot), where visitors could get a peek into the future. He worked as though he was in a race against time, and in fact, Walt's health was beginning to **deteriorate**. Eventually, X-rays showed that he had lung cancer. A smoker for fifty years, he had an operation to try to correct the damage to his lung, but it didn't work.

The last conversation Walt had with Roy the day before he passed away, on December 15, 1966, was about Epcot. He was always planning the next thing, always excited, right to the very end.

Roy opened Walt Disney World in his brother's memory on October 1, 1971. Epcot,

Magic Kingdom Park in Walt Disney World, with Space Mountain in the background

Some people believe that after Walt Disney's death, his body was frozen so that it could be brought back to life. That's just a rumor. It's not true—or even possible! But it is true that Walt's spirit will live forever through all his creations.

Walt's last dream, opened on October 1, 1982. There is now Disneyland Paris and a Disneyland in Tokyo, Japan. Disney movies are an important part of the culture in the United States and all over the world. That's thanks to Walt's vision and inexhaustible energy. No matter how many obstacles stood in his way, he never gave up and always managed to create magic.

Disney Beyond Walt

No one would accuse Walt of thinking small. No idea was too wild or far-reaching for him. Still, it's hard to imagine even Walt picturing an empire as vast as the one bearing his name. Disney has become a company that reaches clear across the globe with all kinds of entertainment. From TV networks to radio stations to book publishing to apps, Disney does it all. Its music division has produced mega stars such as Demi Lovato, Selena Gomez, and Miley Cyrus—not to mention the whole *High School Musical* franchise with its hit movies, songs, stars, and even stage productions. Meanwhile, Disneyland has mushroomed into eleven theme parks, and forty-three resorts and cruises around the world. But no matter how big Disney gets, animation— Walt's first love—is still at the heart of its business. Disney continues to turn out favorites like *The Lion King* and *Tangled,* with many more sure to come.

Disneyland Paris is the most visited tourist destination in Europe.

10 THINGS YOU SHOULD KNOW ABOUT WALT DISNEY

1 Walt, born December 5, 1901, in Chicago, was one of five children born to Elias and Flora Disney.

2 Walt's family moved around a lot, so as a kid he spent time in the city and on a real farm where the pigs were his responsibility.

3 Walt, who never much cared for school, never got his high school degree.

4 During World War I, Walt, who was only seventeen, signed up to be an ambulance driver and was sent to France.

5 After deciding to become a professional artist, Walt started an animation company called Laugh-O-gram Films.

6 Walt met his future wife, Lillian, when she took a job doing "ink and paint" for his newly created Disney Brothers Studio; the couple eventually had two daughters, Diane and Sharon.

7 One of the first Mickey Mouse cartoons, called *Steamboat Willie*, was also the world's first fully synchronized sound cartoon.

8 Under Walt's direction, Walt Disney Studios made the first full-length animated movie, *Snow White and the Seven Dwarfs*.

9 Walt oversaw the planning and construction for Disneyland, which opened on July 17, 1955.

10 Walt passed away on December 15, 1966, before he could see Walt Disney World or Epcot open to the public.

10 MORE THINGS THAT ARE PRETTY COOL TO KNOW

1 Walt Disney once rode in a buggy with Buffalo Bill when the Wild West Show was in town.

2 Once, in his high school art class, the teacher gave the class a homework assignment to draw the human body. Walt's drawing was so good, the teacher thought he copied it from a book and told him to draw another one in front of the class. He did it perfectly.

3 Walt never had an official title at Walt Disney Studios.

4 During World War II, on D-day, Mickey Mouse was the password at the Allied Supreme Headquarters in Europe.

5 Walt didn't like school, and didn't pay much attention in class. He drew pictures in class instead of doing work. He said once that finishing the seventh grade was the hardest thing he'd ever done.

6 Walt's love of performing, and the attention it got him, led to him coming to school one day dressed as Abraham Lincoln. He even learned the Gettysburg Address by heart. His teacher was thrilled, and the principal let Walt go from class to class so that he could recite it for everyone.

7 Walt won a special Oscar for *Snow White*. The statue was a regular Oscar, but there were seven little statuettes on little steps to represent the dwarfs. Shirley Temple presented it to him, and told him not to be nervous.

8 Walt made a very popular set of nature films called True-Life Adventures.

9 Starting in 1937, Walt produced eighty-one feature-length movies at The Walt Disney Studios.

10 Walt did the voice of Mickey Mouse himself from 1928 until 1946 for all the theater cartoons.

GLOSSARY

Acclaim: praise

Accompaniment: to play along with a singer on a musical instrument

Adversity: a difficult situation that lasts for a long time

Animation: the activity of making movies by using drawings, pictures, or computer graphics

Celluloid: a kind of film used to make movies

Deteriorate: to get worse

Documentary: a movie or television program about real people and events

Entrepreneurial: interest in starting businesses and finding new ways to make money

Illusion: something you see that does not really exist

In sync: when two or more things happen at the same time and speed

Innovation: a new idea or invention

Inspiration: the act of filling someone with an emotion, an idea, or an attitude

Live-action: a movie that is not animated

Mimic: to imitate someone else

Revelation: a very surprising and previously unknown fact that is made known

Transparent: a substance that is clear like glass so that objects on the other side can be seen

Visionary: someone who has the ability to think ahead and plan

PLACES TO VISIT

Create some magic in your life by visiting—either online or in real life—these places that pay tribute to Walt's life and vision.

Disneyland, Anaheim, California

Walt's original theme park has expanded way past the original Sleeping Beauty's castle and

Fireworks are a regular event at Disneyland.

Main Street, U.S.A., to include a second park with attractions from newer Disney movies such as Cars and a bug's life.

disneyland.disney.go.com/parks

Walt Disney World & Epcot, Orlando, Florida

Walt Disney World now sits on more than 30,000 acres in Orlando, Florida, and has four theme parks. The original, Magic Kingdom, harkens back to the classic Disney elements that Walt loved, such as Main Street, U.S.A., Cinderella's Castle, and the Walt Disney Railroad. Epcot, however, is all about real life. The 300-acre park takes visitors not only all around the globe with pavilions dedicated to eleven different countries, but also back and forth in time. In the iconic giant "golf" ball at Epcot's entrance is the attraction Spaceship Earth, which is a tour through 40,000 years of human communication.

disneyworld.disney.go.com

The Walt Disney Family Museum, San Francisco, California

Cofounded by Walt's daughter Diane and grandson Walter E. D. Miller, this 40,000-square-foot museum features drawings and animation

Mickey Mouse's Walk of Fame star in Hollywood, L.A.

from *Walt's early years, recordings of him talking, movies, and a thirteen-foot model of Walt's original vision for Disneyland.*

waltdisney.org

The Walt Disney Hometown Museum, Marceline, Missouri

Visitors to the museum in Walt's hometown will learn the story of his childhood through hundreds of personal letters and items that belonged to him and his family.

waltdisneymuseum.org

BIBLIOGRAPHY

Story of Walt Disney, The: Maker of Magical Worlds, Bernice Selden, Yearling, 1989.

Walt Disney: His Life in Pictures, edited by Russell Schroeder, Introduction by Diane Disney Miller, Disney Press, 1996.

Walt Disney: The Triumph of the American Imagination, Neal Gabler, Knopf, 2006.

Walt Disney: Young Movie Maker (Childhood of Famous Americans), Marie Hammontree, Illustrated by Fred Irvin, Aladdin, 1997.

Who Was Walt Disney?, Whitney Stewart, Illustrated by Nancy Harrison, Grosset & Dunlap, 2009.

INDEX

Also Available:

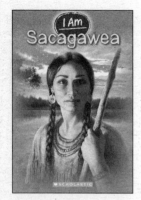

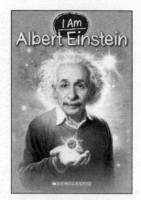

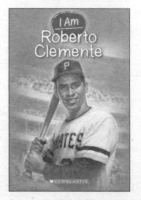